W9-AOP-260

Talking Hands

GREETINGS AND PHRASES

SALUDOS Y FRASES

WRITTEN BY KATHLEEN PETELINSEK AND E. RUSSELL PRIMM
ILLUSTRATED BY NICHOLE DAY DIGGINS

A SPECIAL THANKS TO OUR ADVISERS: JUNE PRUSAK IS A DEAF THERAPEUTIC RECREATOR WHO
BELIEVES IN THE MOTTO "LIFE IS GOOD," REGARDLESS OF YOUR ABILITY TO HEAR.

CARMINE L. VOZZOLO IS AN EDUCATOR WHO WORKS WITH CHILDREN
WHO ARE DEAF OR HARD OF HEARING AND THEIR FAMILIES.

The Child's World

Published in the United States of America by The Child's World®
PO Box 326, Chanhassen, MN 55317-0326
800-599-READ
www.childsworld.com

Cover / frontispiece: left, right—Comstock Images.

Interior: 3, 5, 7, 8, 10, 11, 12, 15—Photodisc; 4, 9, 16, 18, 19, 23—Stockdisc; 6, 14, 21, 22—Comstock Images; 13, 20—RubberBall Productions; 17—Grace / zefa / Corbis.

The Child's World®: Mary Berendes, Publishing Director

Editorial Directions, Inc.: E. Russell Primm, Editorial Director; Katie Marsico, Project Editor and Managing Editor; Caroline Wood, Editorial Assistant; Javier Millán, Proofreader; Cian Laughlin O'Day, Photo Researcher and Selector

The Design Lab: Kathleen Petelinsek, Art Director; Julia Goozen, Art Production

LIBRARY OF CONGRESS CATALOGING-IN-PUBLICATION DATA
Petelinsek, Kathleen.
   Greetings and phrases = Saludos y frases / by Kathleen Petelinsek and E. Russell Primm.
      p. cm. – (Talking hands)
   Summary: Provides illustrations of American Sign Language signs and Spanish and English text for various greetings and phrases.
   In English, Spanish, and American Sign Language.
   ISBN 1-59296-682-9 (lib. bdg. : alk. paper)
   1. American Sign Language—Conversation and phrase books—Juvenile literature. 2. Spanish language—Conversation and phrase books—Juvenile literature. 3. English language—Conversation and phrase books—Juvenile literature. 4. Salutations—Juvenile literature. I. Primm, E. Russell, 1958– II. Title. III. Title: Saludos y frases. IV. Series: Petelinsek, Kathleen. Talking hands.
   HV2476.P4754 2006
   419'.7083461–dc22   2006009036

NOTE TO PARENTS AND EDUCATORS:

The understanding of any language begins with the acquisition of vocabulary, whether the language is spoken or manual. The books in the Talking Hands series provide readers, both young and old, with a first introduction to basic American Sign Language signs. Combining close photo cues and simple, but detailed, line illustration, children and adults alike can begin the process of learning American Sign Language. In addition to the English word and sign for that word, we have included the Spanish word. The addition of the Spanish word is a wonderful way to allow children to see multiple ways (English, Spanish, signed) to say the same word. This is also beneficial for Spanish-speaking families to learn the sign even though they may not know the English word for that object.

Let these books be an introduction to the world of American Sign Language. Most languages have regional dialects and multiple ways of expressing the same thought. This is also true for sign language. We have attempted to use the most common version of the signs for the words in this series. As with any language, the best way to learn is to be taught in person by a frequent user. It is our hope that this series will pique your interest in sign language.

Hi/Hello.
Hola.

1.

2.

Index finger of flat right hand touches forehead. Move hand away from head.

Tocar la frente con el dedo índice derecho y la mano plana. Mover mano hacia afuera.

3

Goodbye.
Adios/Hasta luego.

 1.

Bend fingers (which are pressed together) up and down.

Doblar dedos (opuestos) hacia arriba y abajo.

What's your name?
¿Como te llamas?

1.

2.

3.

4.

Flat right hand faces out. Both hands make the "H" hand shape. Bottom of right middle finger taps top of left index finger. Move both hands in and out at the same time.

Mano derecha plana hacia afurea. Las dos manos forman la "H." El dedo medio derecho golpetea arriba del dedo índice de la mano izquierda. Mover las dos manos hacia adentro y afuera al mismo tiempo.

My name is . . .
Me llamo . . .

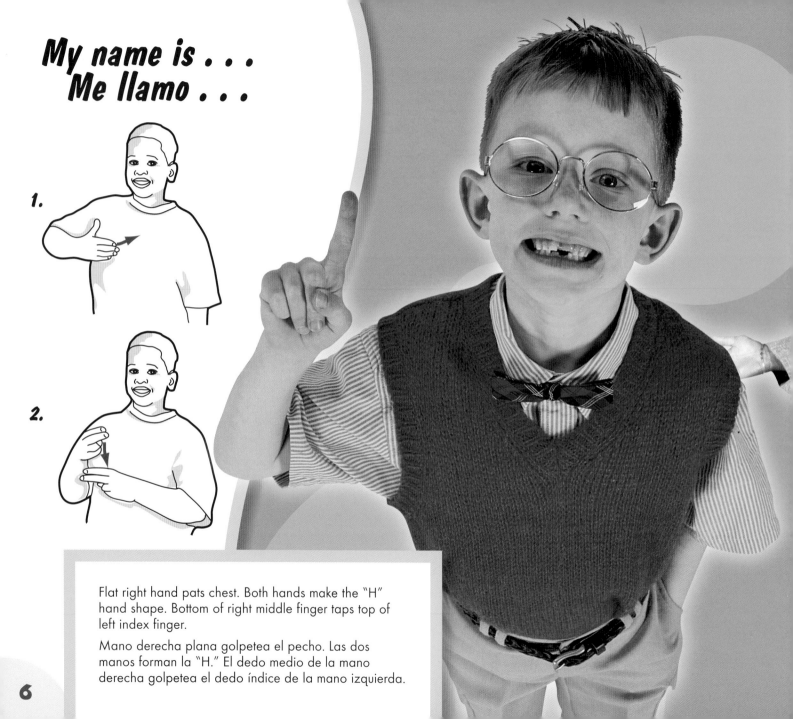

1.

2.

Flat right hand pats chest. Both hands make the "H" hand shape. Bottom of right middle finger taps top of left index finger.

Mano derecha plana golpetea el pecho. Las dos manos forman la "H." El dedo medio de la mano derecha golpetea el dedo índice de la mano izquierda.

Nice to meet you.
Encantado(a) de conocerte.

1.

2.

3.

Palm of flat left hand is up. Palm of flat right hand is down. Left hand stays still while right hand slides off. Both hands make the "1" hand shape and move toward each other and touch. Point right index finger outward.

Palma izquierda plana hacia abajo. Palma derecha plana hacia abajo. La mano izquierda se mantiene sin mover mientras la mano derecha se desliza de el. Las dos manos forman el "1" y convergen. El dedo índice apunta hacia afuera.

How are you?
¿Como estas?

1.

2.

3.

Bend fingers of both hands with fingertips pointing toward chest.
Rotate hands so fingertips point up. Point right index finger outward.

Doblar dedos de las dos manos con las yemas de los dedos
apuntando hacia el pecho. Rotar las manos. El dedo índice apunta
hacia afuera.

I'm fine.
Estoy bien.

1.

2.

Right index finger taps chest. Open right hand (with palm facing left). Tip of right thumb taps chest twice.

El dedo índice de la mano derecha golpetea el pecho. Abrir la mano derecha (palma hacia la izquierda). La yema del pulgar golpetea dos veces.

9

Please.
Por favor.

1.

Right hand should be flat and touching chest. Make a circular movement on chest.

Mano derecha plana toca el pecho. Mover la mano en forma circular sobre el pecho.

Thank you.
Gracias.

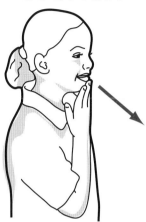

1.

2.

Flat right hand moves down and away from chin.

La mano derecha plana hace movimiento lineal hacia abajo de la barbilla.

You're welcome.
De nada.

1.

2.

Flat right hand moves toward stomach.

Mover la mano derecha plana hacia el estómago.

Excuse me.
Con permiso.

1.

2.

Fingertips of bent right hand slide off flat left hand. Right index finger taps chest.

Doblar las yemas de la mano derecha en forma de garra y deslizar sobre la mano izquierda. El dedo índice derecho golpetea el pecho.

13

Yes.
Sí.

1.

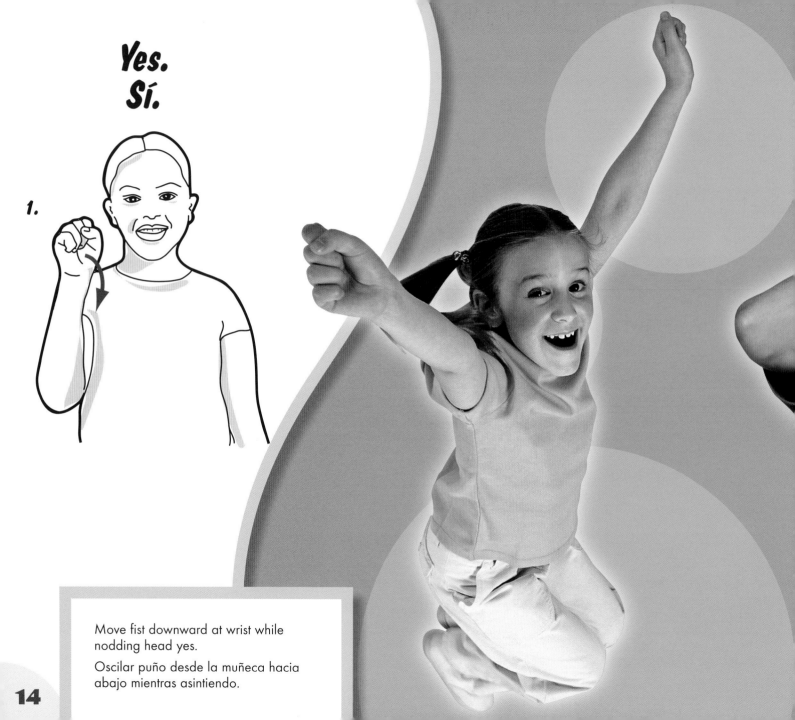

Move fist downward at wrist while nodding head yes.

Oscilar puño desde la muñeca hacia abajo mientras asintiendo.

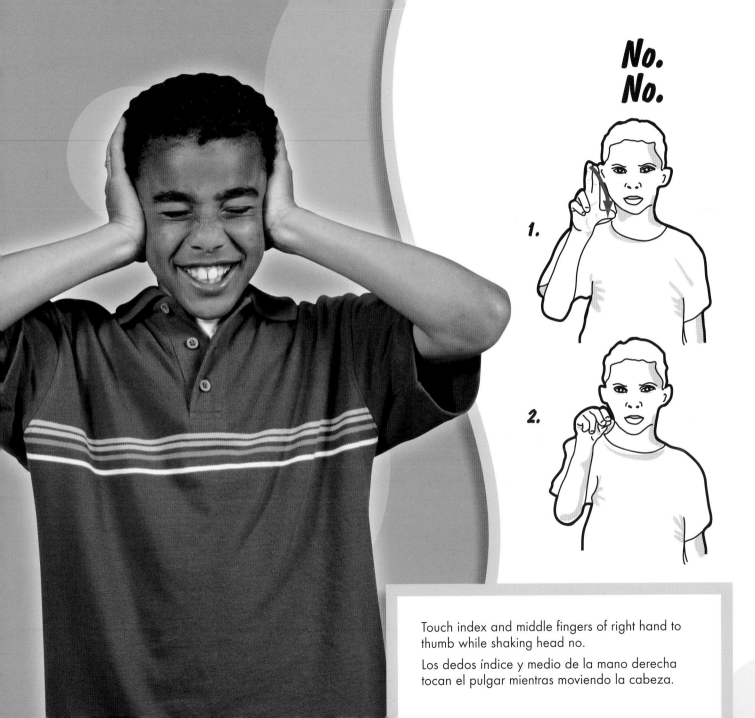

No.
No.

1.

2.

Touch index and middle fingers of right hand to thumb while shaking head no.

Los dedos índice y medio de la mano derecha tocan el pulgar mientras moviendo la cabeza.

I'm sorry.
Lo siento.

1.

Right hand makes the "A" hand shape and makes a circular movement on chest.

Formar la "A" con la mano derecha y hacer movimiento circular sobre el pecho.

What time is it?
¿Que hora es?

1.

2.

Right hand makes the "X" hand shape and taps back of left wrist twice. Both hands are open. Slightly move both hands in and out at the same time.

Formar la "X" con la mano derecha y golpetear la muñeca izquierda dos veces. Las dos manos abiertas. Movimiento ligero hacia adentro y afuera a la misma vez.

17

I like you.
Me gustas.

1.
2.
3.
4.

Right index finger taps chest. Thumb and middle finger touch chest. Thumb and middle finger close as hand moves away from body. Point index finger outward.

El dedo índice derecho golpetea pecho. Los dedos pulgar y medio tocan el pecho. Los dedos pulgar y medio convergen a la vez que la mano se aleja del cuerpo. El dedo índice apunta hacia afuera.

Help!
¡Ayuda!

1.

Right fist (with extended thumb) is pushed up by flat left hand.

Puño derecho (pulgar extendido) empujar hacia arriba con la mano izquierda plana.

Come with me.
Ven conmigo.

1.

As right arm moves toward body, wrist bends.

A la vez que el brazo derecho converge con el cuerpo, doblar la muñeca.

Good morning.
Buenos dias.

1.

2.

3.

Both hands are flat. Right hand moves downward from chin to palm of left hand. Left hand is placed on the inside of right elbow. Right hand arcs up and toward body.

Las dos manos están planas. Mover mano derecha hacia abajo desde la barbilla a la palma de la mano izquierda adentro del codo derecho. Mano derecha inclinada hacia arriba y hacia el cuerpo.

Good afternoon.
Buenas tardes.

1.

2.

Both hands are flat. Right hand moves downward from chin. Right arm is angled out and away from body. Index finger of left hand touches right elbow.

Las dos manos están planas. Mover mano derecha hacia abajo desde la barbilla. Brazo derecho en ángulo y alejado del cuerpo. El dedo índice izquierdo toca el codo derecho.

Good night.
Buenas noches.

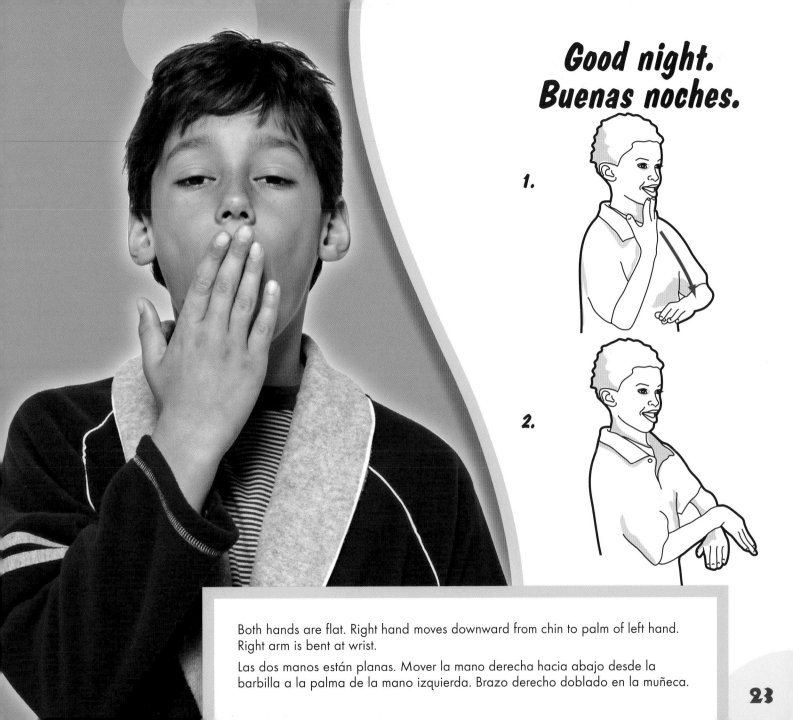

1.

2.

Both hands are flat. Right hand moves downward from chin to palm of left hand. Right arm is bent at wrist.

Las dos manos están planas. Mover la mano derecha hacia abajo desde la barbilla a la palma de la mano izquierda. Brazo derecho doblado en la muñeca.

A B C D E F

G H I J K

L M N O P

Q R S T U

V W X Y Z

Alina is seven years old and is in the second grade. Her favorite things to do are art, soccer, and swimming. DJ is her brother!

Dareous has seven brothers and sisters. He likes football. His favorite team is the Detroit Lions. He also likes to play with his Gameboy and Playstation.

DJ is eight years old and is in the third grade. He loves playing the harmonica and his Gameboy. Alina is his sister!

24